Logical Reasoning

Book 5

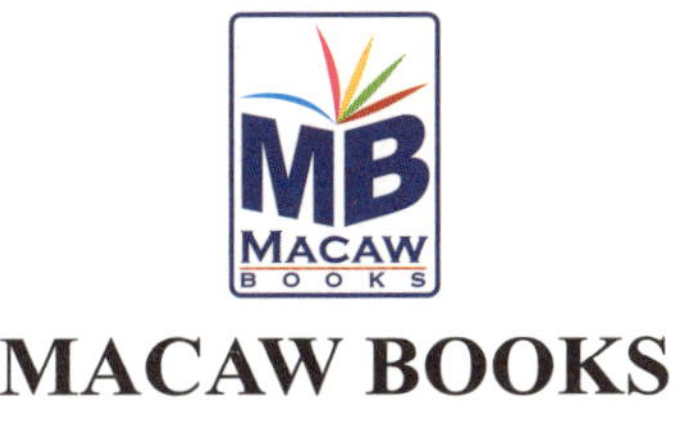

MACAW BOOKS
www.macawbooks.com

shop online @
www.macawbooksonline.com

Published by Macaw Books

ISBN 978-1-60346-293-8
www.macawbooks.com

Printed in India

Contents

1 Age Puzzles

Q1. Solve the mathematical age problems below and tick the correct option:

Example: Jack is 15 years old. His mother's age is 3 times his age. How old is Jack's mother?

a) 35 years

b) 40 years

c) 45 years

d) 50 years

Answer: Jack's age is 15 years. Her mother's age is 3 times his age, i.e., 15 x 3 = 45. Thus, Jack's mother is 45 years old.

Hence, the correct option is: c) 45 years

1. A is 12 years old and B is 2 years older than C. If C is 3 years older than A, how old is B?

   a) 12 years b) 15 years c) 16 years d) 17 years

2. Tom is 20 years old. If Jim is 5 years older than Tom and 4 years younger than Kim, how old is Kim?

   a) 29 years b) 30 years c) 16 years d) 25 years

3. I am just 5 times as old as my daughter. If my daughter's age is 5 years, what is my age?

   a) 20 years b) 25 years c) 30 years d) 15 years

4. Tim, Pim and Kim are cousins. Tim is 8 years old. Pim is thrice as old as Tim. Kim is half as old as Pim. How old is Kim?

   a) 10 years b) 16 years c) 12 years d) 15 years

5. A is 11 years old. B is 4 years older than C and 3 years younger than A. How old is C?

a) 4 years b) 5 years c) 6 years d) 8 years

6. Jerry is 10 years old. His mother is 5 times as old as him. His father is 6 years older than his mother. What is the age of Jerry's father?

a) 50 years b) 56 years c) 60 years d) 70 years

7. Betty's father is 49 years old. He is seven times as old as Betty. How old will be Betty in three years from now?

a) 5 years b) 7 years c) 10 years d) 14 years

8. Mona is 46 years old. Her friend Shawn is 10 years younger to her. Mona's son Jerry is half as old as Shawn. How old is Jerry?

a) 15 years b) 18 years c) 20 years d) 12 years

9. Anna is the daughter of Mary. Anna is 15 years old. Mary is four times as old as Anna. How old was Mary when Anna was born?

a) 55 years b) 60 years c) 50 years d) 45 years

10. P is 14 years old. P's brother Q is 4 years older than her. P's mother, R, is three times as old as Q. How old is R?

a) 50 years b) 52 years c) 54 years d) 56 years

Q2. Read the passage below and answer the questions that follow:

A, B, C, D, E, F, G, H, I, J, K and L are workers of a company. A is 25 years old and B is twice as old as A. C is 5 years younger to B. D and E are of the same age. F is 3 years younger to A and one year elder to E. G and J are twice the age of D. H is 6 years older to C. I is thrice the age of F. L is one-sixth the age of I. K is half the age of I.

Example: What is the age of B?

a) 40 years
b) 50 years
c) 60 years
d) 70 years

Answer: A is 25 years old and B is twice the age of A, i.e., 25 x 2 = 50. Therefore, B is 50 years old. Hence, the correct option is: b) 50 years

1. What is the age of C?

   a) 45 years b) 40 years c) 35 years d) 38 years

2. What is the age of F?

   a) 20 years b) 21 years c) 22 years d) 23 years

3. What will be the age of E after 5 years?

   a) 21 years b) 24 years c) 23 years d) 26 years

4. What was the age of D 15 years ago?

   a) 4 years b) 5 years c) 6 years d) 7 years

5. By how many years is G older than E?

   a) 15 years b) 18 years c) 21 years d) 24 years

6. By how many years is H older to B?

a) 0 years b) 1 year c) 2 years d) 3 years

7. What is the age of K?

a) 25 years b) 28 years c) 30 years d) 33 years

8. By how many years is A older to L?

a) 14 years b) 10 years c) 15 years d) 12 years

9. What will be the age of I after 7 years?

a) 70 years b) 72 years c) 73 years d) 71 years

10. By how many years is J younger to C?

a) 2 years b) 3 years c) 4 years d) 5 years

2 Number Series

Q1. Read the number series below. Look for the degree and direction of change between the numbers and find what number should come next:

Example: 3, 1, $\frac{1}{3}$, $\frac{1}{9}$, ...

a) $\frac{1}{10}$ b) $\frac{1}{12}$ c) $\frac{1}{18}$ d) $\frac{1}{27}$

Answer: It is a division series. The numbers are divided by 3 repeatedly to get the next number.

$\frac{6}{3} = 3$

$\frac{3}{3} = 1$

$\frac{1}{3} = \frac{1}{3}$

$\frac{\frac{1}{3}}{3} = \frac{1}{9}$

$\frac{\frac{1}{9}}{3} = \frac{1}{27}$ Hence, the correct option is: d) $\frac{1}{27}$

1. 36, 34, 35, 33, 34, 32, ...

   a) 30 b) 31 c) 29 d) 33

2. 66, 67, 65, 68, 69, 65, 70, ...

   a) 65 b) 72 c) 71 d) 69

3. 25, 5, 1, $\frac{1}{5}$, $\frac{1}{25}$, ...

   a) $\frac{1}{50}$ b) $\frac{1}{100}$ c) $\frac{1}{75}$ d) $\frac{1}{125}$

4. 1, 2, 4, 7, 11, 16, ...

   a) 20 b) 22 c) 24 d) 25

5. 0, 5, 15, 30, 50, ...

a) 75 b) 60 c) 100 d) 125

6. 99, 90, 82, 75, 69, ...

a) 60 b) 62 c) 64 d) 65

7. 1,1, 2, 6, 24, 120, ...

a) 720 b) 700 c) 240 d) 500

8. 2, 10, 2, 15, 2, 20, 2, 30, ...

a) 1 b) 2 c) 40 d) 50

9. 720, 657, 594, 531, 468, ...

a) 460 b) 407 c) 405 d) 400

10. 850, 800, 825, 775, 800, 750, ...

a) 725 b) 800 c) 700 d) 775

Q2. Identify the pattern and choose the pair of numbers that comes next:

Example: 30, 25, 33, 22, 36, 19, 39, ...

a) 42, 15 b) 42, 16 c) 16, 42 d) 16, 40

Answer: It is an alternating subtraction series of numbers. There are two different patterns shown. In the first pattern, 3 is added to every alternating number. In the second pattern, 3 is subtracted from every alternating number.

Pattern 1: 30 + 3 = 33, 33 + 3 = 36, 36 + 3 = 39, 39 + 3 = 42

Pattern 2: 25 – 3 = 22, 22 – 3 = 19, 19 – 3 = 16

Hence, the correct option is: c) 16, 42

1. 6, 20, 8, 14, 10, 8, 12, ...

   a) 2, 14 b) 14, 2 c) 16, 4 d) 4, 14

2. 1, 2, 3, 4, 5, 6, 7, 8, ...

   a) 10, 9 b) 9, 10 c) 9, 11 d) 10, 11

3. 100, 50, 95, 55, 90, 60, 85, ...

   a) 60, 80 b) 80, 60 c) 65, 80 d) 80, 65

4. 7, 13, 14, 26, 21, 39, 28, ...

   a) 35, 52 b) 42, 52 c) 52, 42 d) 52, 35

5. 6, 600, 18, 300, 54, 150, 162, ...

   a) 125, 486 b) 486, 125 c) 75, 486 d) 486, 75

Q3. Look carefully for the pattern in the following series. Tick (✓) the pair of numbers that comes next:

Example: 60, 58, 56, 53, 51, 49, 46 ...

a) 43, 41 b) 44, 41 c) 44, 42 d) 43, 40

Answer: It is an alternating subtraction series. There are two numbers being subtracted. 2 is subtracted twice and then 3 is subtracted once.
60 – 2 = 58, 58 – 2 = 56, 56 – 3 = 53, 53 – 2 = 51,
51 – 2 = 49, 49 – 3 = 46, 46 – 2 = 44, 44 – 2 = 42
Hence, the correct option is: c) 44, 42

1. 5, 9, 13, 18, 23, 27, 31, ...

   a) 35, 40 b) 36, 41 c) 35, 39 d) 36, 40

2. 9, 18, 27, 37, 46, 55, 65, 74, ...

   a) 83, 93 b) 84, 94 c) 84, 93 d) 83, 92

3. 70, 64, 58, 52, 45, 39, 33, ...

   a) 21, 27 b) 27, 21 c) 20, 27 d) 27, 20

4. 680, 645, 600, 565, 520, 485, ...

   a) 450, 415 b) 450, 405 c) 440, 405 d) 440, 395

5. 120, 180, 240, 290, 350, ...

   a) 410, 460 b) 400, 460 c) 400, 450 d) 410, 470

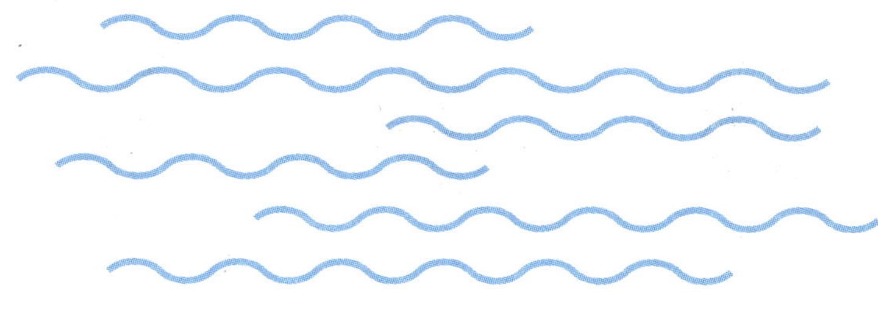

3 Clockwise and Counterclockwise

Q1. **Look at the pictures below. Try to determine the position of these objects on being turned clockwise or counterclockwise. Tick (✓) the correct option:**

Example:  **Quarter turn clockwise**

a) 

b) 

c) 

d) 

Answer: Quarter turn clockwise means 90 degrees to the right ↷.
Therefore, the correct option is:

d) 

  Quarter turn counterclockwise

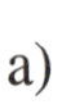
a)  b)  c)  d) 

2 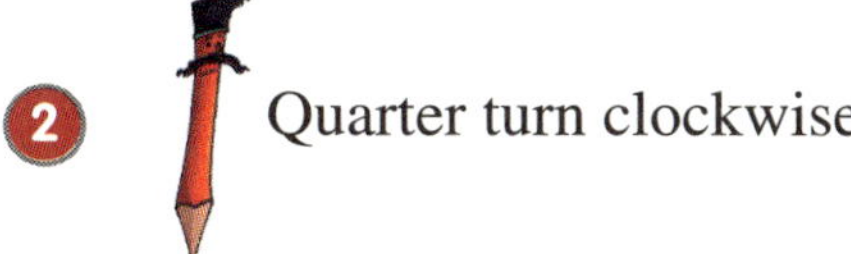 Quarter turn clockwise

a) 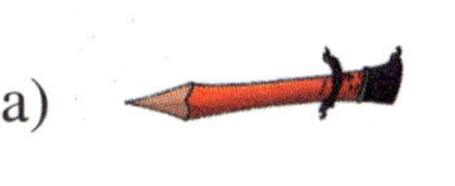 b)  c)  d)

3  Quarter turn counterclockwise

a)  b)  c) d) 

4  Quarter turn clockwise

a) 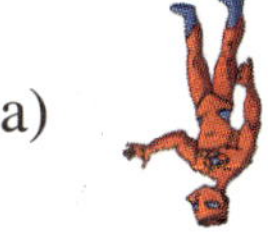 b)  c)   d) 

5  180 degrees counterclockwise

a)   b)  c)  d) 

6 180 degrees clockwise

a)  b)  c)  d) 

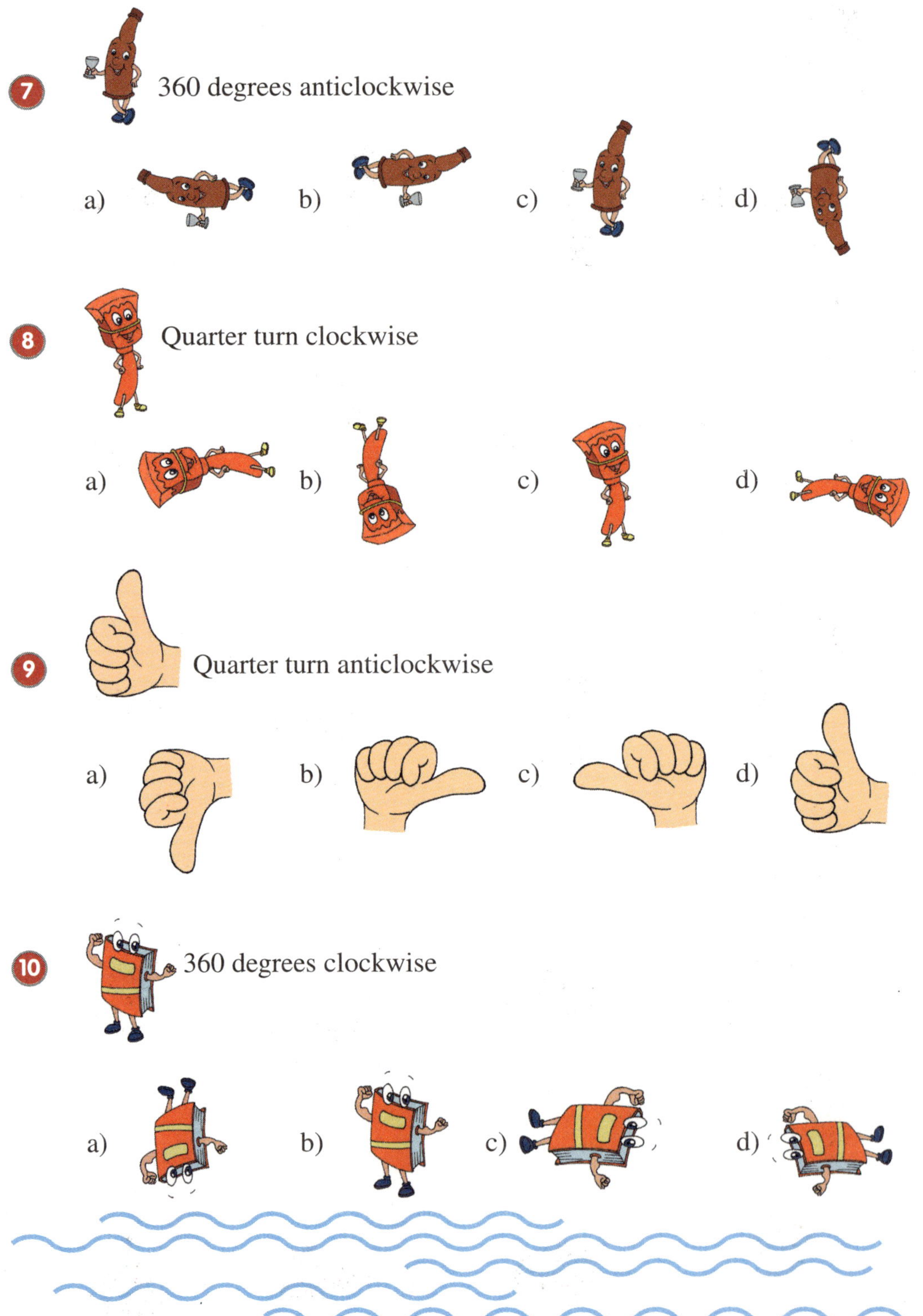

7 360 degrees anticlockwise

a) b) c) d)

8 Quarter turn clockwise

a) b) c) d)

9 Quarter turn anticlockwise

a) b) c) d)

10 360 degrees clockwise

a) b) c) d)

4 Coding and Decoding

General Smith and General Marshal decided to send coded messages to each other. They prepared the following code:

Letter	A	B	C	D	E	F	G	H	I	J	K	L	M
Code	1	2	3	4	5	6	7	8	9	/	@	$	&

Letter	N	O	P	Q	R	S	T	U	V	W	X	Y	Z
Code	*	+	=	|	}	<	;	>	{	!	\	^	%

Q1. Choose the correct code for the following messages:

Example: Hide under the bush

a) 8549>*45} ;85 2><8

b) 8549>*54} ;85 2><8

c) 8945>*45} ;85 2><8

d) 8945>*54} ;85 8><2

Answer: On coding the message 'hide under the bush' using the table above, we get the option: c) 8945 >*45} ;85 2><8

1. Fire your gun

a) 69}%+^}> *>*

b) 96}% +^}> 7>*

c) 96}% ^+>} 7>*

d) 69}5 ^+>} 7>*

2. Be careful

a) 25 31}56>$ b) 25 31}56>$

c) 25 31}65>$ d) 25 31}65>$

3. Run fast

a) }>* 61<; b) }>* 61>;

c) }>* 16<; d) }>* 16>;

4. Do not shout

a) 4+ *+; <4+>; b) 4+ *+; >8+<;

c) 4+ *+; <+8>; d) 4+ *+; <8+>;

5. Kill the enemy

a) @9$$;58 5*5&^ b) @9$$;85 5*5&^

c) @9$$;58 8*8&^ d) @9$$;85 8*8&^

Q2. Decode the following messages using the table given in the previous page. Tick the right option.

Example: 1; ;85 69}<; 7$1*35

a) at the first dance
b) at the first chance
c) at the first glance
d) at the first trance

Answer: On decoding the message 1; ;85 69}<; 7$1*35 using the table above, we will get the option: c) at the first glance

1. 1; =1<;

a) at last b) at blast

c) at past d) at vast

2. 1}5 ^+> ;89}<;^

a) Are you thirsty
b) Are you nasty
c) Are you thirty
d) Are you nerdy

3. 75;;9*7 =19}54

a) Getting scared
b) Getting blared
c) Getting spared
d) Getting paired

4. ^+> 1}5 1 &+*@5^

a) You are a monkey
b) You are a donkey
c) You are a swanky
d) You are a honky

5. 9 81{5 1 =5*

a) I have a hen
b) I have a den
c) I have a ten
d) I have a pen

Q3. Choose the correct code:

Example: If BEE is coded as 277 and ANT is coded as 543, how is BAT coded ?

a) 253 b) 732 c) 577 d) 532

Answer:

B	E	E
2	7	7

A	N	T
5	4	3

B	A	T
2	5	3

Hence, the correct option is: a) 253

1. RAT is coded as *#5

CAT is coded as X#5

How is CAR coded ?

a) *#X
b) X#*
c) #X*
d) *X#

2. PAN is coded as 123

   BOWL is coded as 4567

   EGG is coded as 899

   How is APPLE coded?

   a) 29978 b) 21187 c) 27718 d) 21178

3. TOOL is coded as %^^#

   How is LOOT coded?

   a) #%^^ b) #^%^ c) #^^% d) #^^#

4. TO is coded as 34

   ILL is coded as 788

   NAP is coded as 165

   How is TIN coded?

   a) 765 b) 371 c) 173 d) 317

5. BOOK is coded as 7**9

   LOCK is coded as #*39

   How is BLOCK coded?

   a) 7#*39 b) 7*#39 c) 7#**9 d) 7#*93

Q4. Decode the words and tick the correct option:

Example: If 456 is the code for CAR and 137 is the code for TOY, 4561 is the code for?

a) CART b) PART c) TART d) FART

Answer:

4	5	6
C	A	R

1	3	7
T	O	Y

4	5	6	1
C	A	R	T

Hence, the correct option is: a) CART

1. *35 is the code for TAX

   4677 is the code for FULL

   8912 is the code for SEND,

   435 891* is the code for?

   a) FAX WENT b) FAX SENT c) FAX CENT d) FAX RENT

2. If #5* is the code for HOT

   768* is the code for BRAT

   758* is the code for ?

   a) COAT b) BOSS c) BOAT d) BOOT

3. 5274 is the code for RAMP

   8*1*9* is the code for DELETE,

   95*29 is the code for ?

   a) TREES b) TREAT c) TRIPS d) GREET

4. 7856 is the code for LEFT,

   5876 is the code for ?

   a) HELD b) FEEL c) FELT d) FEAR

5. 123456 is the code for MOTHER,

   1265 is the code for ?

   a) MOAN b) MOAT c) MOST d) MORE

5 Letter and Symbol Series

Q1. Choose the right option to fill in the blanks.

Example: APL, BRO, CTR, ______, EXX

a) DUV

b) DVU

c) VDU

d) DVV

Answer: There are 3 alphabetical series.
Series 1: The letters are in alphabetical order-A, B, C, D, E
Series 2: The letters are in alphabetical order with a letter skipped in between – P, R, T, V, X
Series 3: The letters are in alphabetical order with two letters skipped in between – L, O, R, U, X
Hence, the correct option is: b) DVU

1. ACD, CCE, ECF, _____, ICH

   a) GCH b) CGG c) GCG d) GGC

2. W1X, X2Y, Y3Z, ____, A5B

   a) A4Z b) Z4A c) Z3A d) Y4Z

3. MAB. OCD, QEF, ____, UIJ

   a) SGH b) SHG c) RGH d) TGH

4. AXBY, CXDY, EXFY, _____, IXJY

   a) HXGY b) GYHX c) GXIY d) GXHY

5. FST, HTS, JST, ___, NST

a) LST b) LTS c) MTS d) MST

6. PG3, Q8H, RI13, ___, TK23

a) SJ18 b) S16J c) S18J d) SJ16

7. VUT, TSR, RQP, ___, NML

a) QPO b) OPN c) PNO d) PON

8. HYI, JWK, LUM, _____, PQQ

a) NSO b) NTO c) OSN d) OTN

9. ACF, FHK, KMP, ___, UWZ

a) PQU b) PQT c) PRU d) PRT

10. B2E, E5H, H8K, ___, N14Q

a) K11N b) K11M c) K12N d) K10N

Q2. Study the pattern and complete the series. Tick (√) the correct option:

Example:

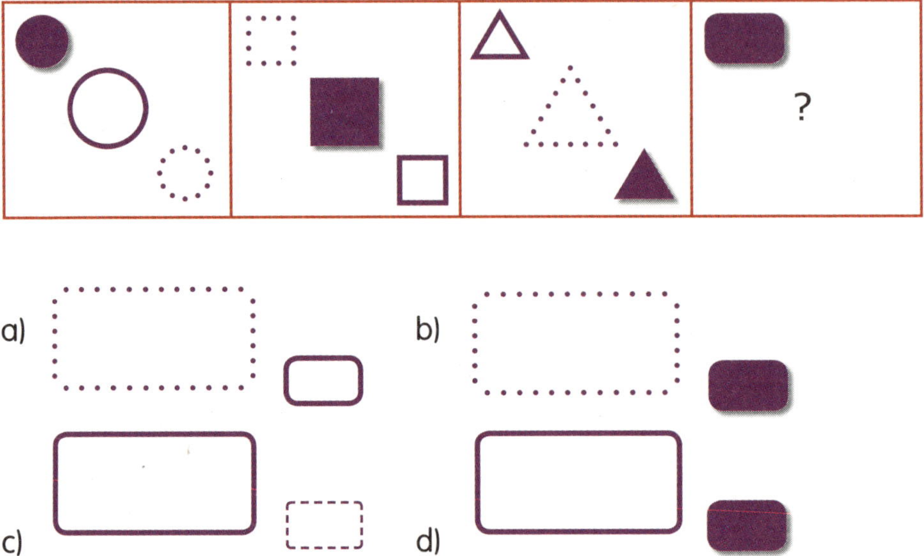

Answer: In each part, the size of all the shapes is similar but the shading differs. The shading is shifting towards right, in the pattern: 123, 312, 231 and 123. The shading pattern in the 1st part will repeat itself in the 4th part. Hence, the correct option is: c)

1. A∢A, ⋗A⋗, ∀⋗∀, ∢ ?

a) ∀ A

b) ∀ ∢

c) ⋗ ∢

d) ∢ ∀

2  ?

a) 

b)

c)

d)

3 ?

a)

b)

c)

d)

4  ?

a)

b)

c)

d)

5 

a)

b)

c)

d)

6 ЕШЗ, ШЗШ, ЗШЕ, Ш ?

a) Е Ш

b) З Ш

c) Ш З

d) Е Е

7 ↑ ↗ →, ↗ → ↘, → ↘ ↓, ↘ ?

a) ↙ ↓

b) ↘ ↓

c) ↓ ↙

d) ↓ ↘

8 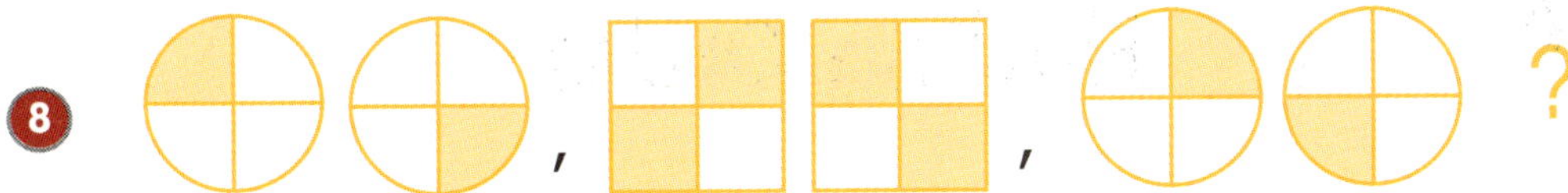

a) 

b) 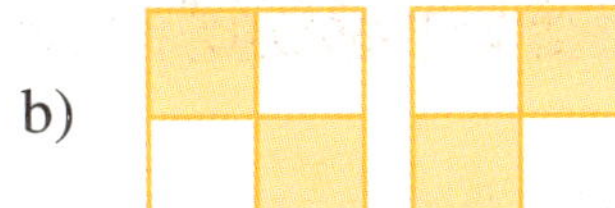

c) 

d) 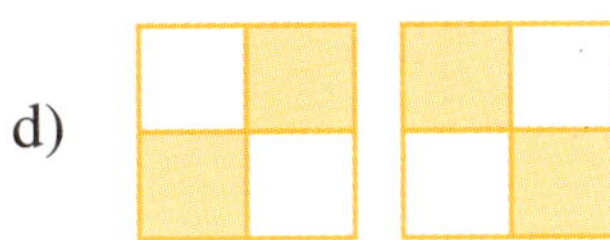

9 B B B B, B B B B, B B B B, B B ?

a) B B

b) B B

c) B B

d) B B

10 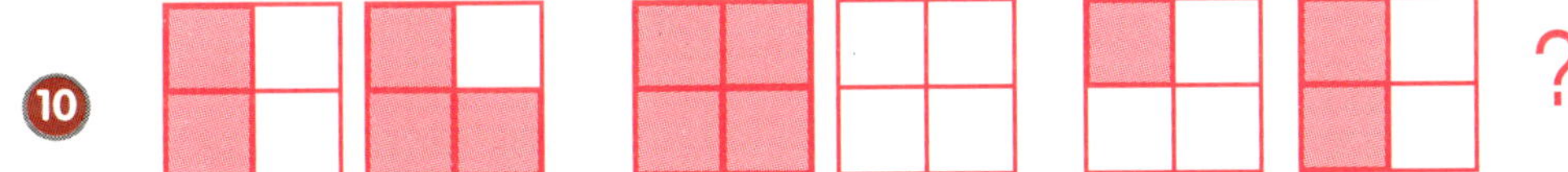

a) 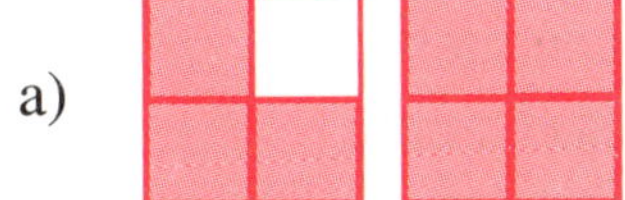

b) 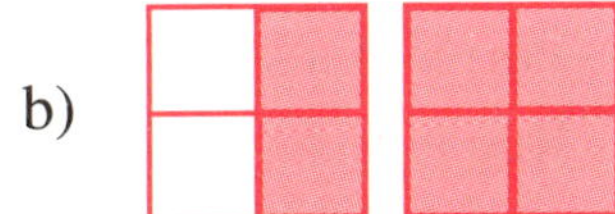

c)

d)

6 Finding Order

Q1. Read the passage below and answer the questions that follow:

Example: A does not live closer to the hospital than B, B lives farther from the hospital than C. Who lives closest to the hospital?

a) A b) B c) C d) None

Answer: A does not live closer to the hospital than B. Therefore, B lives closer to the hospital than A. Again, B lives farther from the hospital than C. Therefore, C lives closer to the hospital than B.
Thus, C lives closest to the hospital. Hence, the correct option is: c) C

1. Tom's school is smaller than Jerry's school but larger than Kim's school. Whose school is the smallest?
   a) Tom's school
   b) Kim's school
   c) Jerry's school
   d) Tony's school

2. Sarah is younger than Phony. Phony is older than Zara. Zara is younger than Sarah but older than Tim. Who is the youngest amongst all?
   a) Sarah
   b) Tim
   c) Phony
   d) Zara

3. The green house is shorter than the yellow house. The purple house is taller than the red house. The green house is taller than the purple house. Which house is the tallest?
   a) Purple house
   b) Green house
   c) Red house
   d) Yellow house

4. The dance club has more members than the drama club. The painting club has fewer members than the cricket club. The cricket club has fewer members than the dance club. Which club has the fewest members?
   a) The cricket club
   b) The dance club
   c) The painting club
   d) The drama club

5. P's annual salary is more than T's annual salary. R's annual salary is more than P's annual salary. S's annual salary is more than R's annual salary. Whose annual salary is the least amongst all?

a) P's annual salary	b) T's annual salary
c) R's annual salary	d) S's annual salary

6. The plum cake is larger than the chocolate cake. The strawberry cake is larger than the plum cake. The vanilla cake is larger than the chocolate cake but smaller than the plum cake. Which cake is the smallest amongst all?

a) Vanilla cake	b) Strawberry cake
c) Plum cake	d) Chocolate cake

7. The yellow marble is farther from the target than the red marble. The blue marble is closer to the target than the red marble. The green marble is farther from the target than the blue marble. Which marble is farthest to the target?

a) Yellow marble	b) Green marble
c) Red marble	d) Blue marble

8. The watch is more expensive than the shirt and the tie. The tie is less expensive than the shirt but more expensive than the shoes. Which of the following is the least expensive item amongst all?

a) Tie	b) Shoes
c) Shirt	d) Watch

9. During a cricket match, player A scored fewer points than player B. Player D scored fewer points than player A. Player C scored more points than player A but less points than player B. Who scored the highest?

a) Player D	b) Player C
c) Player B	d) Player A

10. The Mill city is shorter than the Mall city. The Ramp city is larger than the Gold city but smaller than the Mall city. Which city is the largest amongst all?

a) The Gold city	b) The Mill city
c) The Ramp city	d) The Mall city

Q2. Read the passages below and answer the questions that follow:

Example: What is the 50th letter in the passage below?

Humpty Dumpty sat on a wall,
Humpty Dumpty had a great fall.
All the King's horses, and all the King's men
Couldn't put Humpty together again!

a) A b) L c) K d) E

Answer: Count the letters until you reach the 50th letter. The second L is the 50th letter. Hence, the correct option is: b) L

1. What is the 42nd letter in the passage below?

The lightning and the thunder
They go and come;
But the stars and the stillness
Are always at home.

a) T b) H c) E d) U

2. What is the 40th letter in the passage below?

Little Boy Blue, come blow your horn;
The sheep's in the meadow, the cow's in the corn.
Where is the boy who looks after the sheep?
He's under the haystack, fast asleep.

a) B b) O c) Y d) N

3. What is the 34th letter in the passage below?

One, two, three, four, five,
Once I caught a fish alive.

Six, seven, eight, nine, ten,
But I let it go again.
Why did I let it go?
Because it bit my finger so.
Which finger did it bite?
The little one upon the right.

a) E b) T c) S d) F

4 What is the 55th letter in the passage below?

Hark, hark, the dogs do bark!
The beggars are coming to town!
Some in rags and some in tags,
And some in velvet gowns.

a) G b) O c) E d) L

5 What is the 36th letter in the passage below?

Twinkle, twinkle, little star,
How I wonder what you are.
Up above the world so high,
Like a diamond in the sky.
Twinkle, twinkle, little star,
How I wonder what you are!

a) H b) W
c) A d) T

7 Reason Better

Q1. Each passage consists of three statements. Based on the first two statements the third statement may be true, false or uncertain. Tick (✓) the correct option below:

Example: Gmail runs faster than Yahoo.
Hotmail runs faster than Gmail.
Yahoo runs faster than Hotmail.
If the first two statements are true, the third statement is?

a) True
b) False
c) Uncertain

Answer: The first two statements are true, thus we have:
Gmail > Yahoo
Hotmail > Gmail
thus, Hotmail > Gmail > Yahoo
Hence, the third statement must be false.

1. I am older than my brother.
My sister is older than me.
My brother is younger than my sister.
If the first two statements are true, the third statement is?
a) True b) False c) Uncertain

2. Apples cost more than bananas.
Bananas cost more than oranges.
Oranges cost more than apples.
If the first two statements are true, the third statement is?
a) True b) False c) Uncertain

3. All the books in the library are in English.
Some of the books in the library are novels.

All the novels in the library are in English.

If the first two statements are true, the third statement is?

a) True b) False c) Uncertain

4 During the past year, Sara shopped more than Kim.

Kim shopped less than Anna.

Anna shopped more than Sara.

If the first two statements are true, the third statement is?

a) True b) False c) Uncertain

5 All the roses in my garden are red.

All the tulips in my garden are white.

All the flowers in my garden are either red or white.

If the first two statements are true, the third statement is?

a) True b) False c) Uncertain

6 Class VI has more boys than Class VII.

Class VIII has fewer boys than Class VII.

Class VI has fewer boys than Class VIII.

If the first two statements are true, the third statement is?

a) True b) False c) Uncertain

7 John is younger than Peter.

Mathew was born after John.

Peter is older than Mathew.

If the first two statements are true, the third statement is?

a) True b) False c) Uncertain

8 Bertha is taller than Betty.

Ben is taller than Betty.

Bertha is taller than Ben.

If the first two statements are true, the third statement is?

a) True b) False c) Uncertain

9. The temperature on Friday was higher than on Saturday.
The temperature on Sunday was higher than on Friday.
The temperature on Saturday was lower than on Sunday.
If the first two statements are true, the third statement is?
a) True b) False c) Uncertain

10. Chocolate has more calories than candies but fewer calories than ice cream.
Candies have more calories than custard but fewer calories than cakes.
Out of the all, custard has the least amount of calories.
If the first two statements are true, the third statement is?
a) True b) False c) Uncertain

11. I sit behind my best friend Joe.
My neighbour sits behind me.
Joe sits behind my neighbour.
If the first two statements are true, the third statement is?
a) True b) False c) Uncertain

12. Three apples cost the same as two oranges.
Five oranges cost the same as one watermelon.
An apple is more expensive than a watermelon.
If the first two statements are true, the third statement is?
a) True b) False c) Uncertain

8 Puzzles

Q1. Identify the pattern and choose the right option.

Example:

A_5	D_8	G_{11}
M_{20}	P_{23}	?
T_{33}	W_{36}	Z_{39}

a) S_{25} b) S_{26} c) R_{25} d) R_{26}

Answer: The letters are in alphabetical order with two letters skipped in between. And the difference between the two consecutive numbers is 3. Therefore, the correct option is: b) S_{26}

1.

Z_{15}	Y_{18}	X_{33}
Q_{110}	P_{20}	?
J_{43}	I_{56}	H_{99}

a) O_{130} b) O_{90} c) R_{90} d) R_{130}

2.

2	6	6
12	8	4
?	48	24

a) 20 b) 21 c) 24 d) 25

3

P_2	Q_2	R_2
M_4	N_5	O_{10}
T_8	U_{10}	?

a) V_{20} b) W_{160} c) V_{90} d) W_{80}

4

2	3	12
3	3	18
4	2	?

a) 8 b) 16 c) 18 d) 20

5

Y_{12}	A_6	?
X_{40}	Z_{10}	B_4
Q_{12}	S_4	U_3

a) B_6 b) C_2 c) B_2 d) C_6

Q2. Identify the pattern and choose the right option.

Example:

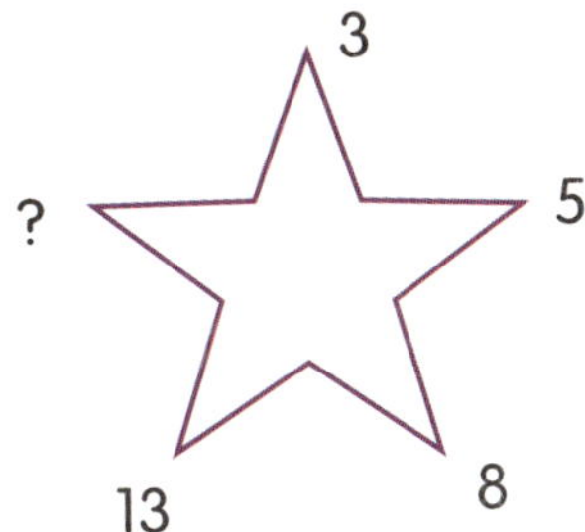

a) 29 b) 22 c) 24 d) 20

Answer: Study the pattern below:

$3 \times 2 - 1 = 5$

$5 \times 2 - 2 = 8$

$8 \times 2 - 3 = 13$

$13 \times 2 - 4 = 22$

Therefore, the correct option is : b) 22

1

a) 37 b) 13 c) 15 d) 10

2

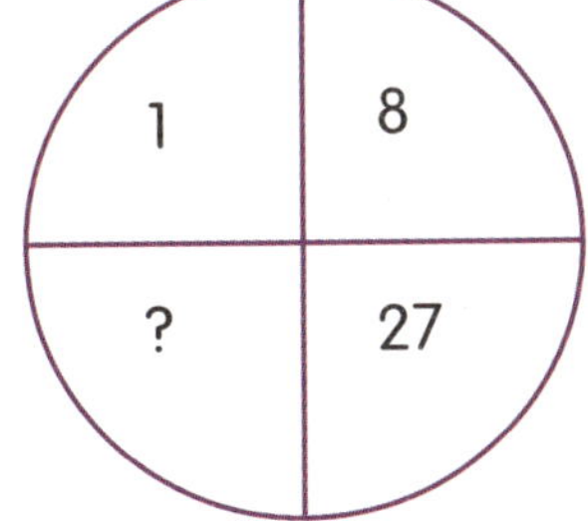

a) 35 b) 42 c) 30 d) 64

3

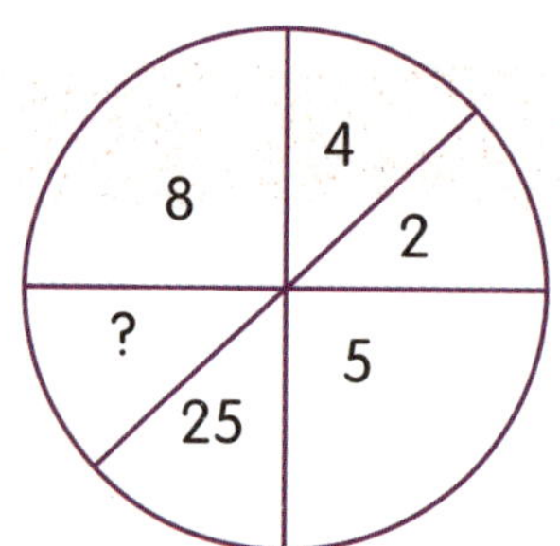

a) 59 b) 125 c) 75 d) 625

4

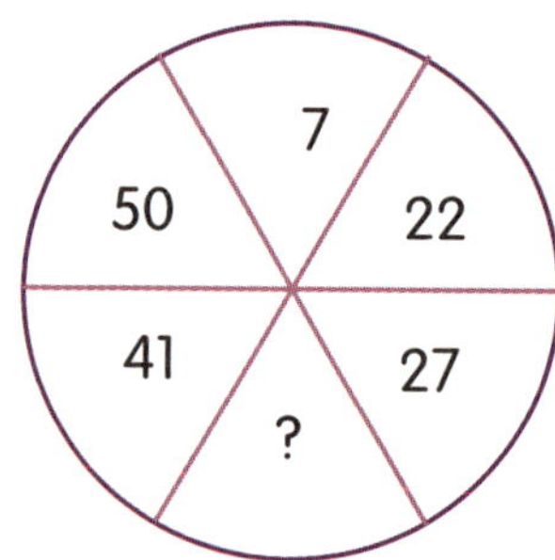

a) 32 b) 38 c) 36 d) 40

5

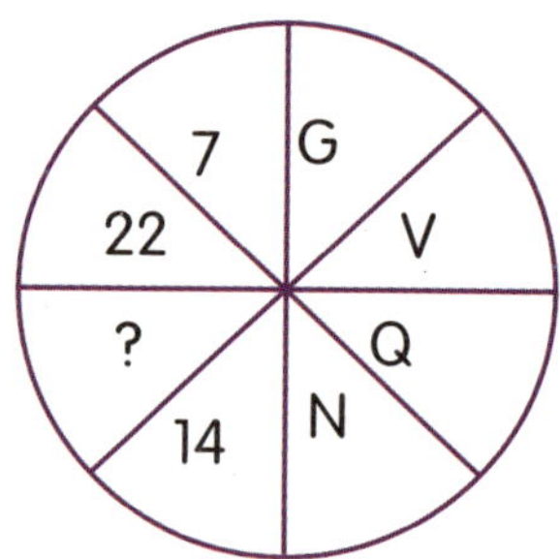

a) 12 b) 13 c) 17 d) 15

Q3. Identify the pattern and choose the right option.

Example:

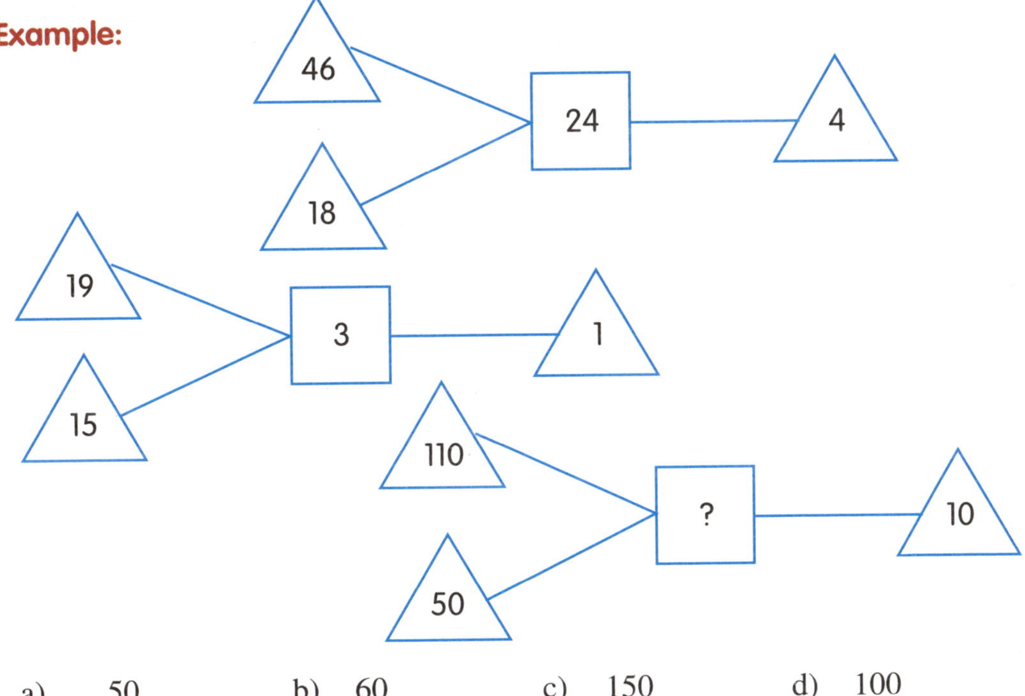

a) 50 b) 60 c) 150 d) 100

Answer: The pattern is:

46 - (18 + 4) = 24

19 - (15 + 1) = 3

Therefore, 110 - (50 + 10) = 50

Hence, the correct option is: a) 50

1

6 1 → 217

2 7 → ?

2 4 → 308

a) 259 b) 300 c) 351 d) 343

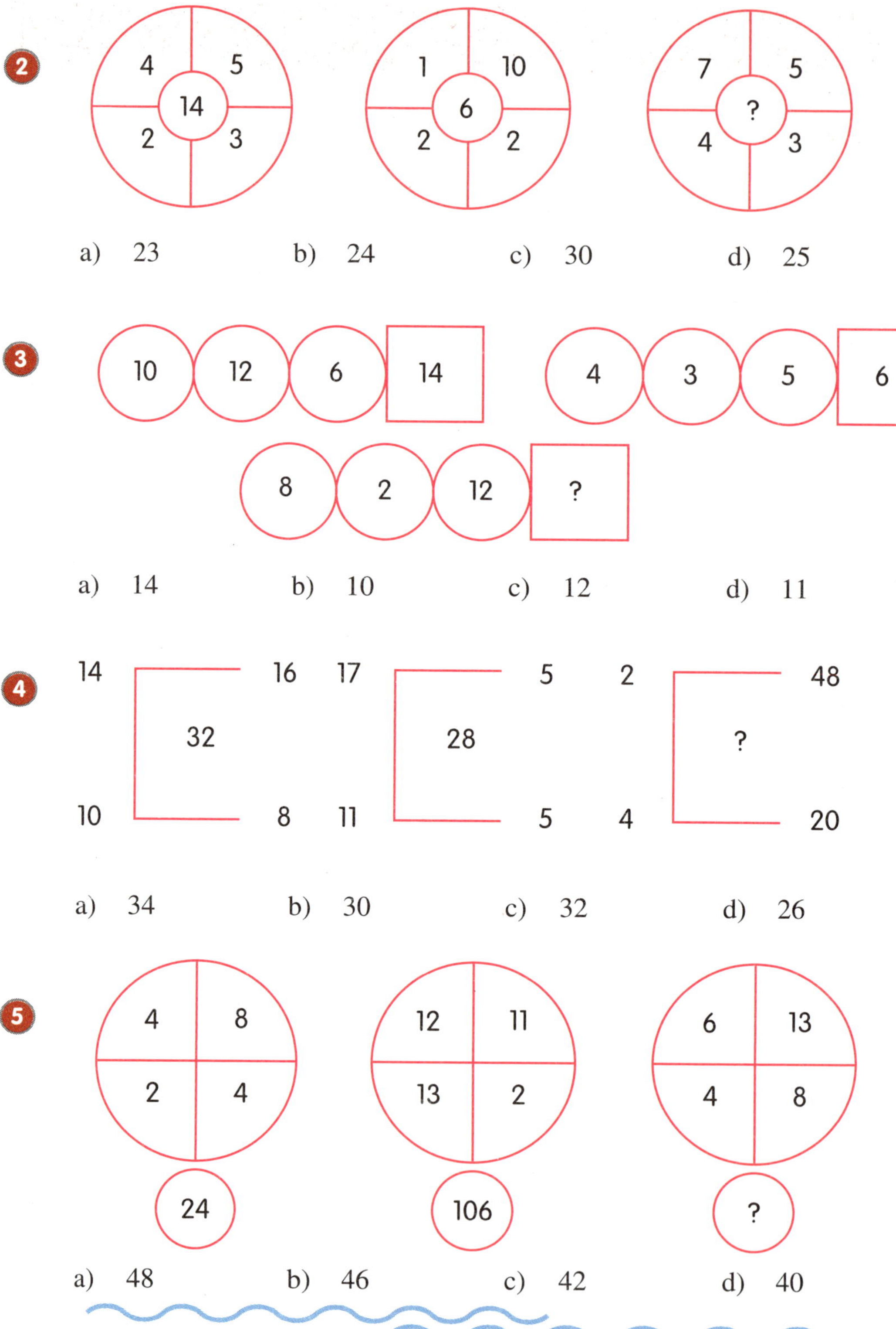
2
4
5
14
2
3
1
10
6
2
2
7
5
?
4
3
a) 23
b) 24
c) 30
d) 25
3
10
12
6
14
4
3
5
6
8
2
12
?
a) 14
b) 10
c) 12
d) 11
4
14
16
32
10
8
17
5
28
11
5
2
48
?
4
20
a) 34
b) 30
c) 32
d) 26
5
4
8
2
4
24
12
11
13
2
106
6
13
4
8
?
a) 48
b) 46
c) 42
d) 40

9 Analogies

Q1. In each of the following questions, the first two words are related to each other. From the options available, find the word that shares the same type of relation with the third word.

Example: Sculptor : Statue :: Architect : ?

a) Fashion
b) Art
c) Building
d) Poetry

Answer: A sculptor makes statues. Similarly, an architect designs buildings. Therefore, the correct option is: c) Building

1. Cricket : Sports :: Spanish : ?

   a) Spain
   b) Language
   c) Knowledge
   d) English

2. Drummer : Musician :: Comedian : ?

   a) Actor
   b) Artist
   c) Man
   d) Funny

3. Water : Boat :: Air : ?

   a) Ship
   b) Bicycle
   c) Car
   d) Aeroplane

4. Umpire : Cricket :: Referee : ?

   a) Football
   b) Hockey
   c) Chess
   d) Cricket

5. Sugar : Sweet :: Tear : ?

   a) Water
   b) Salty
   c) Liquid
   d) Sour

Q2. Choose the correct option for the following analogies:

Example: Twenty-three is to twenty-two as eight is to ________
a) Nine b) Six c) Seven d) Five

Answer: As twenty-three is to twenty-two, eight is to seven. Hence, the correct option is: c) Seven

1. Three is to nine as five is to _______

a) Fifteen b) Ten

c) Twenty d) Twenty-five

2. Eight is to twenty-four as nine is to _________

a) Thirty b) Twenty-seven

c) Thirty-six d) Forty

3. Fifty is to hundred as hundred is to ____________

a) Twenty b) Two hundred

c) One hundred and fifty d) Seventy-five

4. Two is to eight as ten is to __________

a) Thousand b) Hundred

c) Forty d) Sixteen

5. One is to ninety-nine as hundred is to __________

a) One hundred and ninety-eight b) One hundred and ninety

c) Nine hundred and ninety-nine d) Nine hundred

Q3. Choose the correct option to replace the question mark:

Example: MIKE: NJLF :: HAND: ?

a) NDAH b) GZMC c) GBOE d) IBOE

Answer: As MIKE is to NJLF; plus 1 alphabet.

M --------- N
I ------------ J
K ----------- L
E ----------- F

Similarly, HAND is to; plus 1 alphabet.

H ----------- I
A ---------- B
N ---------- O
D ---------- E

Therefore, the correct option is: d) IBOE

1. RAT: TAR :: FOG: ?

   a) GFO b) GOF c) OGF d) FGO

2. SNAKE: NSAEK :: GREEN: ?

   a) RGENE b) RGEEN c) NEERG d) NEEGR

3. APPLE: DSSOH :: ORANGE: ?

   a) RONAEG b) RUEQJG c) RUDQJH d) RUEPKI

4. YELLOW: ZDMKPV :: BLUE: ?

   a) AMTD b) CKVD c) CMVF d) AKTD

5. DELITE: ETILED :: FLOWER: ?

   a) LFWORE b) LFWORE c) OLFREW d) REWOLF

10 Relationships

Q1. Answer the questions below:

Example: Introducing a man, a woman said, "His mother is the only daughter of my mother." How is the woman related to the man?

a) Grandmother
b) Mother
c) Sister
d) Daughter

Answer: The woman said "his mother is the only daughter of my mother". It means she is talking about herself.
Therefore, the correct option is: b) Mother.

1. Pointing at a photograph, Tom said, "She is the wife of the only nephew of the only brother of my mother." How is the lady related to Tom?

   a) Daughter b) Sister c) Wife d) Mother

2. Pointing to a man, Jerry said, "He is the son of the only son of my grandfather." How is the man related to Jerry?

   a) Brother b) Father c) Uncle d) Grandson

3. A is the brother of B, B is the sister of C, C is the father of D. How is A related to D?

   a) Father b) Nephew c) Uncle d) Brother

4. D's son B is married to A whose brother C is married to F, the sister of B. How is C related to D?

   a) Daughter b) Son c) Daughter-in-law d) Son-in-law

5. Pointing to a boy, Tim said, "He is the only son of the only child of my grandfather." How is Tim related to that boy?

   a) Sister b) Son c) Mother d) Wife

Q2. Read the questions carefully and choose the correct answer:

Example: A # B means A is the brother of B and A * B means A is the husband of B. Which of the following indicates that P is the brother-in-law of R?

a) P # Q * R
b) P * R # Q
c) R * P # Q
d) Q # P * R

Answer: P # Q means P is the brother of Q.
Q * R means Q is the husband of R.
Therefore, the option which indicates P is the brother-in-law of R is:
a) P # Q * R

1. A $ B means A is the son of B and A % B means A is the mother of B. Which of the following indicates that X is the wife of Z?

   a) Y % Z $ X b) X % Y $ Z

   c) Y % X $ Z d) Z % Y $ X

2. A + B means A is the brother of B, A × B means A is the father of B and A – B means A is the sister of B. Which of the following relation indicates that R is the niece of Q?

   a) Q + P + O – R b) Q + P × R – O

   c) O – R × P + Q d) Q × P + R – O

3. A + B means A is the daughter of B and A – B means A is the brother of B. Which of the following indicates that X is the mother of Z?

   a) X – Y + Z b) X – Y – Z

   c) Z – Y + X d) Z – Y – X

4. A + B means A is the daughter of B, A – B means A is the brother of B, A % B means A is the father of B and A × B means A is the sister of B. Which of the following indicates M is the niece of K?

   a) K – N % L × M b) M × L – N % K

   c) K + M + N % L d) M × L + N – K

5. A + B means A is the brother of B and A × B means A is the father of B. Which of the following indicates that P is the maternal uncle of R?

   a) P + Q × R b) P + R × Q

   c) P × R + Q d) P + Q + R

Q2. Read the questions carefully and choose the correct option:

Example: If X > Y means X is the brother of Y, X < Y means X is the father of Y and X ^ Y means X is the daughter of Y, who is the mother in P < Q > R ^ S?

a) P

b) Q

c) R

d) S

Answer: Answer: P < Q – P is the father of Q.
Q > R – Q is the brother of R.
R ^ S – R is the daughter of S.
Therefore, S and P are the parents of Q and R.

P (father)   S (mother)

Q ⟶ R (daughter)
(brother)

Hence, the correct option is: d) S

1. X % Y means X is the husband of Y, X * Y means X is the granddaughter of Y and X # Y means X is the mother of Y. In A % B # C * D, how is D related to A?

   a) Aunt   b) Mother

   c) Mother-in-law   d) Grandmother

2. If P $ Q means P is the son of Q, P # Q means P is the mother of Q and P * Q means P is the brother of Q, how is B related to D in A # B $ C * D?

   a) Uncle   b) Aunt

   c) Niece   d) Nephew

3. If P * Q means P is the brother of Q, Q ^ R means Q is the son of R, R > S means R is the wife of S and P < S means P is the son of S, how is R related to P?

   a) Aunt b) Grandmother

   c) Mother d) Father

4. If A x B means A is the sister of B, A ^ B means A is the mother of B and A + B means A is the brother of B, how is P related to S in P x Q ^ R + S?

   a) Sister b) Aunt

   c) Mother d) Grandmother

5. If X x Y means X is the daughter of Y, X + Y means X is the father of Y, X % Y means X is the mother of Y and X – Y means X is the brother of Y, how is A related to E in A % B + C – D x E?

   a) Mother-in-law b) Daughter-in-law

   c) Aunt d) Mother

Answers

Q1.

1. d 2. a 3. b 4. c 5. a 6. b
7. c 8. b 9. d 10. c

Q2.

1. a 2. c 3. d 4. c 5. c 6. b
7. d 8. a 9. c 10. b

Chapter 2

Q1.

1. b 2. c 3. d 4. b 5. a 6. c
7. a 8. b 9. c 10. d

Q2.

1. a 2. b 3. c 4. d 5. c

Q3.

1. b 2. a 3. d 4. c 5. a

Chapter 3

Q1.

1. b 2. a 3. d 4. c 5. a 6. d
7. c 8. d 9. c 10. b

Chapter 4

Q1.

1. d 2. b 3. a 4. d 5. b

Q2.

1. c 2. a 3. d 4. a 5. d

Q3.

1. b 2. d 3. c 4. b 5. a

Q4.

1. b. 2. c 3. b 4. c 5. d

Chapter 5

Q1.

1. c 2. b 3. a 4. d 5. b 6. c
7. d 8. a 9. c 10. a

Q2.

1. b 2. a 3. c 4. b 5. a
6. a 7. c 8. b 9. d 10. a

Chapter 6

Q1.

1. b 2. b 3. d 4. c 5. b 6. d

7. a 8. b 9. c 10. d

Q2.

1. a 2. d 3. c 4. b 5. a

Chapter 7

Q1.

1. a 2. b 3. a 4. c 5. c 6. b
7. a 8. c 9. a 10. a 11. b
12. b

Chapter 8

Q1.

1. a 2. c 3. a 4. b 5. b

Q2.

1. a 2. d 3. b 4. c 5. c

Q3.

1. c 2. a 3. d 4. a 5. b

Chapter 9

Q1.

1. b 2. a 3. d 4. a 5. b

Q2.

1. d 2. b 3. b 4. c 5. a

Q3.

1. b 2. a 3. c 4. b 5. d

Chapter 10

Q1.

1. c 2. a 3. c 4. d 5. a

Q2.

1. b 2. b 3. c 4. d 5. a

Q3.

1. b 2. d 3. c 4. b 5. a